Benidorm

GU00986029

EVEREST

Editorial Management: Raquel López Varela

Editorial coordination: Eva María Fernández

Text: Luís Seguí Asín

Photographs: Nano Cañas and Archivo Everest

Diagrams: Mercedes Fernández

Cover design: Alfredo Anievas

Digital image processing: David Aller and Ángel Rodríguez

Translated by: Babyl Traducciones

© EDITORIAL EVEREST, S. A.
Carretera León-La Coruña, km 5 - LEÓN
ISBN: 84-241-0467-6
Legal Deposit: LE. 1.128-2003
Printed in Spain

EDITORIAL EVERGRÁFICAS, S. L.
Carretera León-La Coruña, km 5
LEÓN (Spain)
www.everest.es
Customer service: 902 123 400

Benidorm

The archaeological sites of Tossal de la Cala, the small hill situated in one end of the Poniente beach, constitute a testimony of the human presence in the Ancient Times and in the municipal area, with remains of an Iberian village from between the III and I centuries B.C., whose living was based on fishing, and the beautiful terra-cottas of the head of the Punic goddess Deméter-Coré (more known as Tánit). Rome also left signs of their dominion in the area, with remains of a Roman villa in the Partida del Moralet and fragments of Punic and Roman ships that had shipwrecked in the bay of Benidorm. Benidorm is located in the middle of a bay which is delimited by the Escalera Point (Sierra Helada) and the Finestrat Cove, in the Marina Baja region in the province of Alicante. Communicated by the CN-332 road, the A7 Highway and the train of the Generalitat Valenciana (Autonomical Government), the city is located at a distance of 42 km from the city of Alicante. It's present location was originated due to the medieval defensive necessities of the eastern coastline during the period of the Catalan-Aragón kingdom of Jaime I *The Conqueror,* who took possession of the territory of this area around 1245, and who left great part of the region under the command of admiral Bernat de Sarriá. On the 8th of May 1325 the admiral gives the title of village

Above, Playa de Poniente (Poniente beach), in the background, el Tossal de la Cala.

to Benidorm, and consequently it is when the noble lord builds the castle (destroyed during the Independence war in 1812) and sets up the village of Benidorm, which is established behind a small rocky hill that divides the two most important beaches.

Beginning in 1335 the infante Pere d'Aragó i d'Anjou, acting already as lord of the territory, begins decisively the construction of the village, a task continued by his son Alfons d'Aragó i de Foix.

Fishing was in those times the pillar of the local economy, and with its progress and the improvements done in the defense of the coastline, the village of Benidorm was consolidated, improving also its resources in 1666 with the construction of an irrigation channel which already in 1701 contributed with small volumes of water and which allowed to create an irrigation system in the area and attract people from the region.

In 1740, when the population reached the number of about 216 neighbours and the present church of Sant Jaume (San Jaime) was being built, the patron saint of Benidorm, the Virgin of Suffrage (Virgen del Sufragio) was discovered.

In those days the fishermen of the village obtain international prestige for having been entrusted the installation of almost the totality of the trap-netting system (almadraba) of the Mediterranean: among all the ones that were anchored in the coast of Alicante, the one from Benidorm was the most important, for having reached to achieve the biggest "levantada" (trapping) which provided 35.000 tuna fish of about 15 kg of average weight each fish.

On the next page, Cerro Canfali and Punta de la Escalera.

The trap-nets were fixed fishing nets of 450 metres long and 60 metres in width, with 10 or more fishing boats and about 30 men who spread the nets where the tuna fish were captured at their way through the coastline. The captains were called in Valencian the *arraixos (arráeces* in Spanish).

In 1857 the village has registered 3.720 inhabitants. But the improvement in the communications will allow the growth, shy in the beginning, of a new economical facet: tourism. In 1870 the Virgin of Suffrage spa opens its doors. The construction of the road from Silla to Alicante and the arrival of the railway from Madrid to Alicante will slowly help this industry to grow.

First will arrive the pioneer holiday makers of Alcoy and Madrid, who since 1914 can use a narrow gauge train. Around 1925 the first houses in the area of the Levante Beach are built. After the closure in 1952 of the Almadraba, in 1956 the City Council approves the urban distribution of the village in order to create a city which is conceived for tourist leisure based in

well traced streets and broad avenues, which follow the configuration of the beaches. Their general plan is a worldwide known example of a rising city with green spaces and sufficient distance between the buildings so that residents and visitors do not feel in any moment the typical overwhelming feeling of a city which has a high density of population.

In ten years, the population increased in 129%, and with the opening of the airport of l'Altet, in 1967, the city's growth is spectacular.

Benidorm, now with 65.000 inhabitants, has the capacity to house 400.000 persons in its 155 hotels with more than 35.000 beds; 6.000 aparthotels, with 20.000 beds; and 9 campings, with another 5.000, converting it in the third European city with the biggest lodging capacity. In the last three years, several new hotels have been opened, among which stand out the Meliá, Levante Club, Rincón Garden, Madeira Centro, and the Bali, which with its 186 m of height in 52 floors and 450 rooms is the tallest hotel in Europe and the highest

Panoramic view of the skyscrapers. Foreground, Hotel Bali, background, la Isla de los Periodistas (Island of the Journalists).

Two previous pages, night view of Benidorm.

Different aspects of the boardwalk and
Playa de Levante.

The boardwalk at
Playa de Poniente.

building of the whole Mediterranean coastline. Presently, the hotels of the city always maintain an excellent level of occupation, as much in the summer as in the winter, due mainly to the influx of pensioners, achieving an average annual occupation of 85%.

We will start our tour taking as reference the Canalejas square, from one of the most typical streets of our old quarters, the "Carrer dels Gats"(street of the Cats); a sample of the urban design of the old fishermen's Benidorm.

Left, two views of the church of San Jaime; above, picture of the Virgin of Suffrage.

Climbing the paved stairs, we reach the place where the San Jaime church is, whose origins go back to the XVIII century when Benidorm goes through a notable growth and the city starts to expand with the creation of new streets: Santa Faz, Condestable Zaragoza, Alicante, etc., which make up the present picturesque old quarter of the city.

In the number 5 of the Forn street is the Aquarium, with sharks, crocodiles, turtles and snakes. From the old Benidorm we reach one of the most emblematic places of the city, the castle-viewpoint, known also as the *balcony of the Mediterranean*. In the great rock that divides the two beaches used to be the fortress which served as defense against the attacks of the Argelinian and Berber pirates, during the XIV, XV and XVI centuries.

At a later stage the castle was abandoned, having presently only a few rests of the walls, which lie above the rocks of the viewpoint.

Above, two aspects of the "Balcón del Mediterráneo" (Balcony of the Mediterranean); below, staircase of the castle-viewpoint.

SEE MAP OUR HOTEL SEPT 05
IN
BACK ↓

12

Two views of the beach of Benidorm: below, an impressive "Last Supper" sandcastle.

15

Two previous pages,
view from the viewpoint
on the Canfali bluff.
Background, Playa
de Levante.

From this point you can enjoy of a beautiful panoramic view of the bay and the beaches of Levante and Poniente (East and West), of 2 and 3,5 km of length respectively: together with the beach of Mal Pas, they all have the blue flag given each year since 1985 by the European Foundation of Environmental Education, and they are also accessible for handicapped persons.

Next to the harbour, where we can go down by the stairs of the Mirador, is the small beach of Mal Pas which is protected by the cliffs of the castle and the breakwater of the harbour. It is in this area of the city where all the nautical activities are done and from where we can embark in a boat

to an interesting crossing to the isle of Benidorm, denominated in 1970 as the *Isle of the Journalists.*
Two miles from the coast, the isle occupies 7 ha with a length of 700 metres and whose only buildings are the lighthouse and a small outdoor picnic bar. The isle is a prominent continuation of the partial sinking of the Sierra Helada for seismic effects.

Its vegetation in the interior extends with characteristic specimens of bushes, which include from the amaranth to the marine mauve; in the cliffs, the semprevivum, and in the small beach, poppies, prickly pears and aloe. Thousands of terns and crag martins nest in the northern cliff of the isle, where massive tourist visits could endanger this fauna.

On this page, different views of the port of Benidorm.

On the following page: above, panoramic view of the Playa de Mal Pas; below, in the foreground games and sports on the beach and in the background, Isla de los Periodistas.

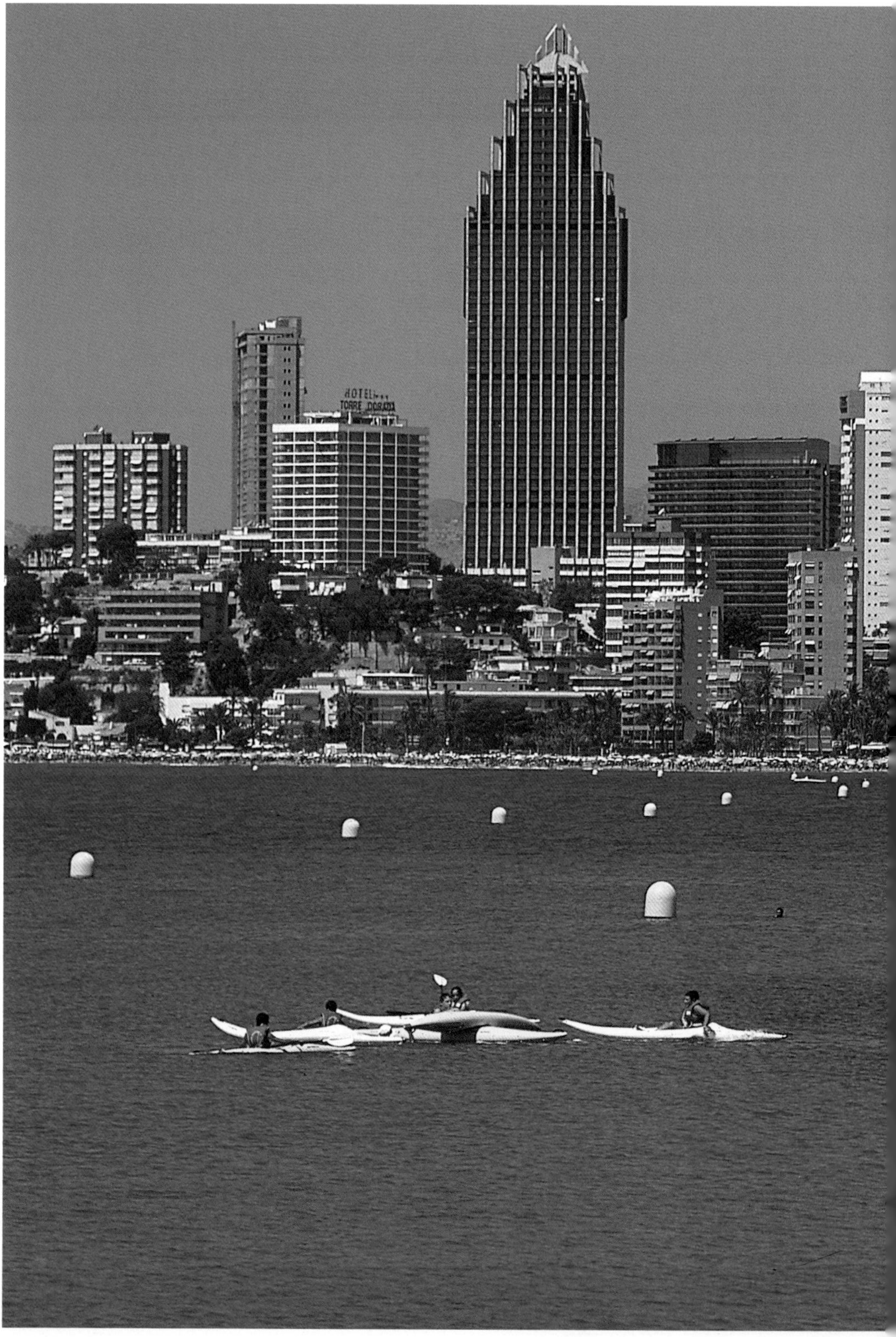
HOTEL
TORRE DORADA

Above, park of L'Aigüera; below, palm grove of the park of Elche.

We contemplate the marine facade of the Poniente Beach, where the Elche park is located, so called because its beautiful palm trees originally were brought from the neighbouring village of the same name.

We will continue our walk through the city, heading to the great lung of Benidorm which is the well known park of L'Aigüera. This great work of urban architecture, designed by Ricardo Bofill, has broad green spaces, a central avenue and the two auditorium where the majority of the artistic and cultural happenings are held, among which stand out the Song Festival of Benidorm, housing besides the Agricultural Museum, which with an oil press, a water wheel and a threshing floor, reveals how people lived in Benidorm before the tourist boom.

Next to the park of l'Aigüera, is the City Council, which has the singularity of the slats of its facade, orientated automatically, they adjust the intensity of the outside light connecting the electrical lighting only when it is necessary. These slats have engraved the name of each one of the 62.000 inhabitants registered in the latest census of the city.

By the pedestrian and commercial avenue of Martínez Alejos we reach the Levante beach, a spectacle for the eye, with a broad seaside promenade between the sand and a row of restaurants and cafeterias with live music every day of the year. At night time is when this great avenue reaches its maximum splendour, turning in to a place of enjoyment and leisure activities for all visitors.

Two previous pages, panoramic view of Benidorm.

22

At the end of the promenade, dominating and protecting Benidorm, is the Sierra Helada, with an extension of 800 ha, it constitutes an interesting natural space for its isolation and proximity to the sea. The whole of this mountain range is scored by roads and tracks, and many trees have been planted there, although we still can find the autochthonous flora which historically has grown in it. It extends parallel to the coast from northeast to southeast. Its length is of 6 km, between the Bombarda Point or of Albir, up to the Pinet Point. Its highest peak is of 438 m and the coast is high, with cliffs of 300 or 400 m and small coves. In the Bombarda Point is located the lighthouse of Altea, and there are remains of watchtowers next to it, as well as in Les Caletes. Several caves formed by the erosion of the sea, such as the Cave of the Lady (Cova de la Dona) or the Pila Cave, open in its seaside slope.

Parallel to the promenade, in the interior is the Avenue of the Mediterranean (avenida del Mediterráneo), with cheerful shops (of the more than 2.500 which has the whole city) and pleasant cafeterias (from a total of 300), where a walk is a real spectacle: it seems that the whole world is within the reach of the bench where the visitor sits for a rest and to observe. A small train runs along this avenue taking the passengers to other places of the city.

In number 8 of this avenue is the Wax Museum, with rooms

Sierra Helada.
Panoramic view of the Punta del Pinet and the cliffs.

dedicated to celebrities, famous painters, terror, American West, cinema and bullfighting.

There are other museums in this avenue, as the museum of Erotic Art, with samples that include periods from 2000 B.C. till the Belle Epoque, of the past century.

Besides there are fun fairs for children, such as Festilandia and Mediterráneo Parc, in the numbers 20 and 29, respectively.

All around there are places where to eat and choose the cuisine of countries of all around the world and with the most varied prices, in the almost 400 restaurants of which Benidorm disposes: there are restaurants of different countries and Spanish regions and of the traditional cuisine of the area, where to savour the typical rice dishes "a banda" and "amb fessols i naps" (with beans and turnips), the "bollos a la paleta" (kind of roll), the "fritanga"... all of which, from the most economic to the most sophisticated of menus are at the visitors disposal. Discotheques, night clubs, disco-bars and live music at the streets assure a very cheerful and animated evening in the city which is the first tourist destination of Spain for the volume of its visitors. To attend the national visitors, the regional houses of all the autonomic communities offer their cuisine and typical shows, for which Benidorm has the most abundant calendar of fiestas of the whole Valencian Community.

Typical dishes: left, putxero de Polop; right, arroz senyoret (a rice dish).

Detailed look at a "falla" in Benidorm.

"Cremá" on the night of March 19.

Leaving the Mediterranean Avenue, we turn left to the Severo Ochoa avenue to reach the big Marine Park Mundomar.
With about 500 animals of different species, such as sea turtles, flamingos, seals, exotic birds, bats, monkeys or iguanas, stands out the aquatic fauna of different places around the world, with areas of penguins and racoons, and the subaquatic vision of the sea lions and dolphins.

Different aspects of the Waterpark Aqualand.

Adjacent to Mundomar is the Aqualand Water Park, which joins its more than ten water chutes to its "Big Band" and "Splash" attractions, for why it is considered one of the most important aquatic parks of the world. In both places attractive restaurants and promenades are open.

In front of these, the Benidorm Palace is a night club of huge dimensions which offers dinner and international variety shows of the best Music Hall that could be seen in any country.

Benidorm, which for its own right has achieved to be distinguished as a first class international tourist resort, receives each year the most diverse kind of tourist flows that arrive from all around the world. Around 4.000.000 tourists confirm, each year, their preference for Benidorm, which continues maintaining its international

leadership in the competitive sector of the tourist offer.

By the Avenue of the Spanish Navy (avenida de la Armada Española) (parallel to the Poniente Beach), the cove of Benidorm has installations of great dimensions, such as the before mentioned building of the hotel Bali.

Going towards Villajoyosa, by the CN 332 road, the Finestrat cove shows hotel complexes, services of all kind and a secluded beach of golden sand protected by the hill of the Tossal which is crowned by the watchtower of Aguiló, from the XVI century, and from where a splendid view of the bay of Benidorm can be seen. Next is the Mediterráneo casino, where the persons keen on gambling can tempt luck with the playing cards, the roulette and the slot machines, and where there is a restaurant of meticulous cuisine and an art gallery.

The following two pages, panoramic view of the cove of Finestrat.

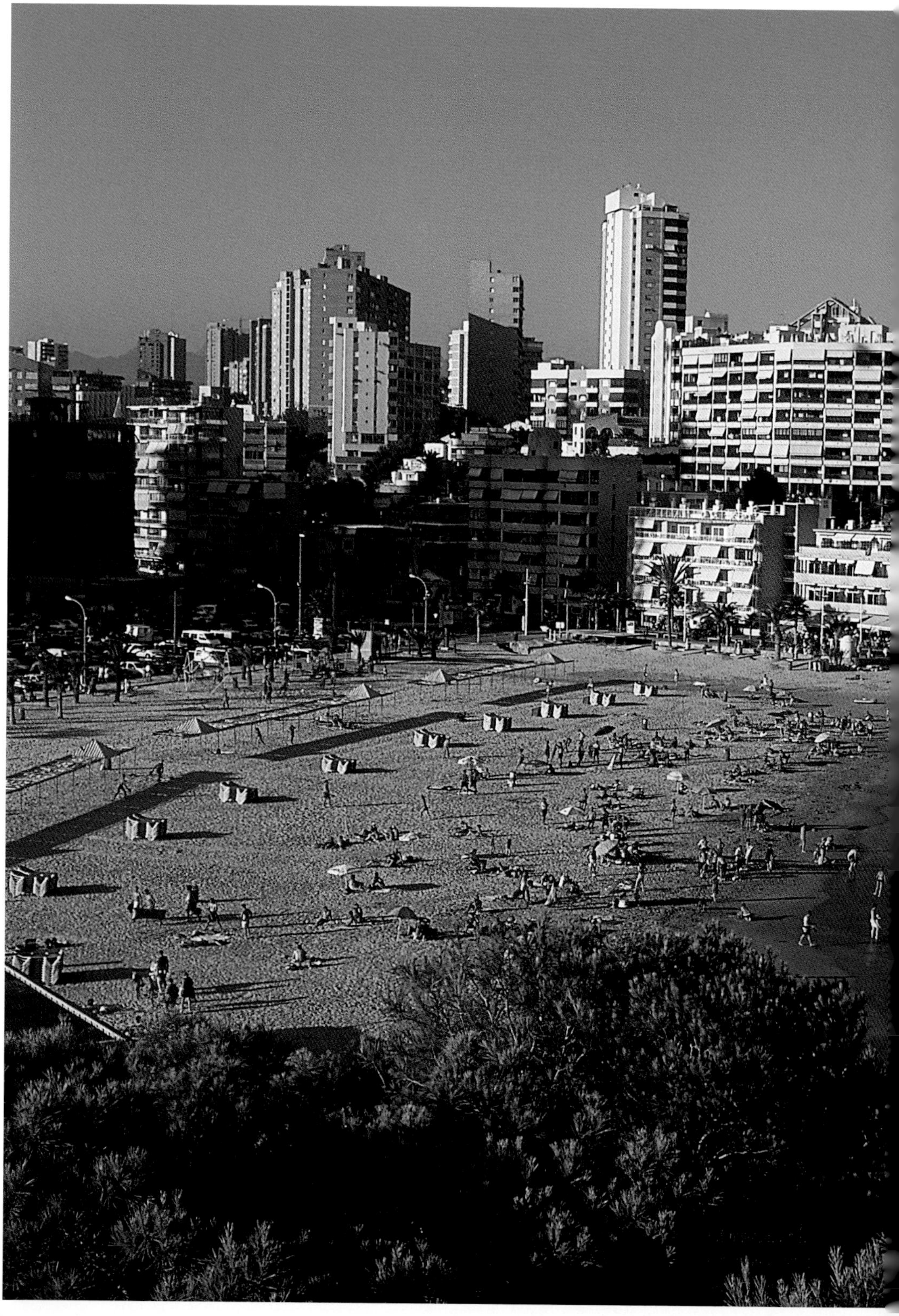

Terra Mítica.
On the following page: above, view of the big lake;
below, Egypt next to the big lake.

From Finestrat and by the 65 A road, we reach Terra Mítica. With an extension of one million square metres, it offers the visitors routes of virtual reality which are identified with the thematic areas of Greece, Rome, Africa, Iberia and the islands, in a great lake which symbolises the Mediterranean sea.

Thanks to this lake, the visitor can move around with Berber rowing boats (jabeques), schooners and vessels through all the bounds of the Park. Each area offers their own shows and different attractions with a similar replica in all cases done for children.

It offers six shows: "the Pyramid", "the Moorish and the Christians", "the Telemaco's Theatre", "Olympia's simulator", "the gladiators of the future" and "the Berber pirates".

Terra Mítica.
"Tizona" the spectacular
inverted rollercoaster.

There are also five mechanic attractions, of which stand out the enormous wooden roller coaster "Magnus Colossus", with more than 1'5 km of length and a height of 50 m; "the Flight of the Phoenix", of 60 m; "the Fury of the Triton", an aquatic splash of 500 m and two big drops, the "Waterfalls of the River Nile", with 549 m; "The Argos Rapids", for a rafting of 500 m; the "Bravo Train", of 1 km; and the last of the installed attractions, the spectacular and vertiginous "Tizona", an inverted roller coaster in an area of nearly 18.000 m², where passengers are hanging from the rails, instead of circulating on top of them. Terra Mítica, which can be visited by 18.000 persons at the same time, is the only theme park of the world that is open in the summer till midnight. It is a pleasant place to have a walk with splendid views and it offers a varied cuisine in any of its 15 restaurants.

Next to Terra Mítica is Terra Natura, opened in 2003, and considered the biggest animal park in Europe, with 32 ha. The park gathers more than 1.500 animals of about 200 different species in an environment which faithfully recreates their natural habitat, with its own original flora adapted to the microclimate of Benidorm. The park is divided in 4 areas: Pangea, America, Asia and Europe, where the animals can be observed through an original system of "zooimmersion".

On the page next to this one: splash at Terra Mítica.

Terra Mítica.
"Cataratas del Nilo" (Niagara Falls),
panoramic view of Benidorm from the rides.

Above, near the spring of Alcántara. On the page next to this one: above, panoramic view of the Sierra Aitana and the impressive Puig Campana (1,406 m); below, view of Finestrat.

On the following two pages: panoramic view of Sella.

Returning to the same previous road, we reach the foothills of the Puig Campana mountain, the second tallest peak of the province of Alicante. With its 1.406 m of height, it stands spectacularly for its proximity to the coast, which is at a distance of 10 km. In the municipal area of Finestrat, the mountain occupies 640 ha, in a rough and rocky formation, of steep slopes, covered with stony areas and magnificent crags. Its most notable characteristic is the gorge of Roldán (tajo de Roldán), which is an enormous fissure in the cresting, also distinguished for having endemic vegetal species. We can reach the mountain from the beautiful village of **Finestrat,** with typical restored houses and cheerful streets where to have a stroll.

Leaving Finestrat we head towards **Sella,** where we will visit the fountain of Alcántara, a village surrounded by limestone mountains of great magnitude and the vertical walls of more than 400 m of height of the Peña de Sella.

We leave Sella and after passing **Relleu,** we reach the harbour of Tudons, where the Safari Park Aitana is located, of two million square metres and at a height of 1.000 m, it is the highest of Europe, and which with a route by car of 7 km takes the visitor among 500 animals which include tigers, lions, giraffes, camels, elephants and other wild animals which are kept in semi-captivity. The park has also didactic routes done by foot in the "Noah's Arch" and a recovery centre for animals of the Iberian fauna. From there we reach the mountain top of **Sierra Aitana,** of 1.558 m, the highest peak of the Valencian Community, where installations of the Spanish Television (RTVE) and the Air Force are placed. Another route to follow is the Callosa d'En Sarriá one, to which we will reach from the Tomas Ortuño street and the Beniardá avenue until we get to the C-3318 road and visit, at a height of 262 m and at a distance of

8 km, La Nucía and Polop (with its fountain of Los Chorros beneath the Ponoch mountain top).

At 4 km is the **Callosa d'En Sarrià,** situated between the Guadalest and Algar rivers, which are the outlets of the Bernia, Aitana and Aixortà mountain ranges.

The abundance of their waters and the fertility of the surrounding grounds have proportioned generous cultivations of almond trees, grapes and even tropical products, such as the kiwi or mango. But it is the loquat, with its own denomination of origin, that personifies the village of Callosa, where half of what is produced of this fruit in Spain is grown and where enormous extensions of greenhouses cover the slopes of the nearby mountains and hills.

Of the historic and present treasures of Callosa we have its monuments: the San Juan Bautista church, the Portal, in the old quarters, the entrance of the Medieval Arch, the remains of the medieval walls and the Convent chapel, where the image of the patron saint, the *Virgen de las Injurias* (Virgin of the Slanders) is kept.

Callosa d'En Sarrià.
Streets and "el Portal"
in the old medieval
neighborhood.

41

Callosa d'En Sarrià. Church of San Juan Bautista.

Different aspects of
Castell de Guadalest.

On the following
two pages, view of
the reservoir from the
Castell de Guadalest
(castle of Guadalest).

Taking the 3313 road, at 12 km, we reach the **Castell of Guadalest,** which has a peculiar and unique belltower built on top of a crag, a real symbol for the second most visited indoor place of Spain after the Prado Museum: two million visitors come each year to Guadalest, which only counts with 200 inhabitants.

At a height of 588 m, the cemetery, located in the castle of Sant Josep, and the manor house of the Orduña, are recommended places to visit. Also worthwhile visiting are the parish church and the Moorish fortress called Alcozaiba, on top of the Alcalá and Cullerot crags.

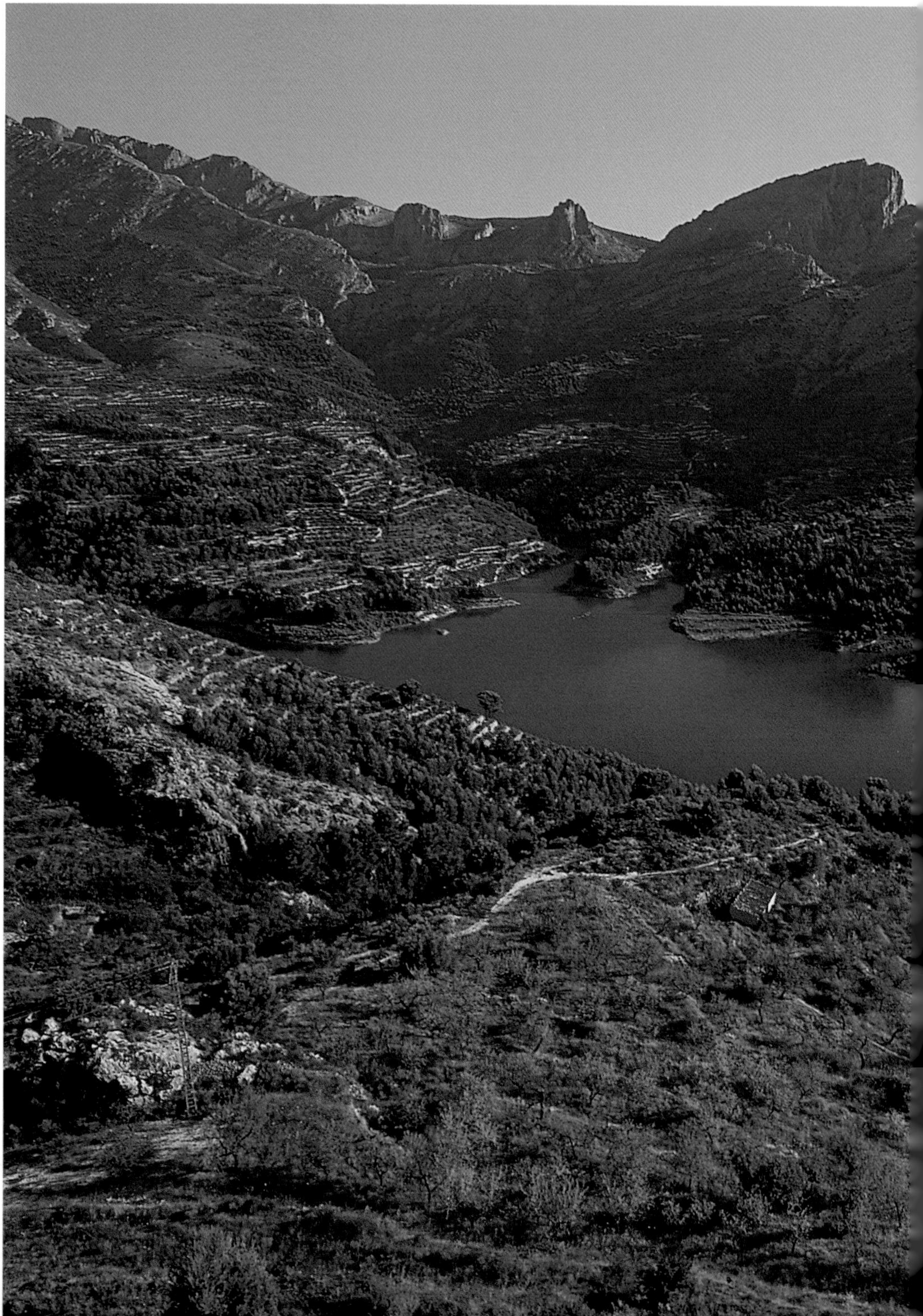

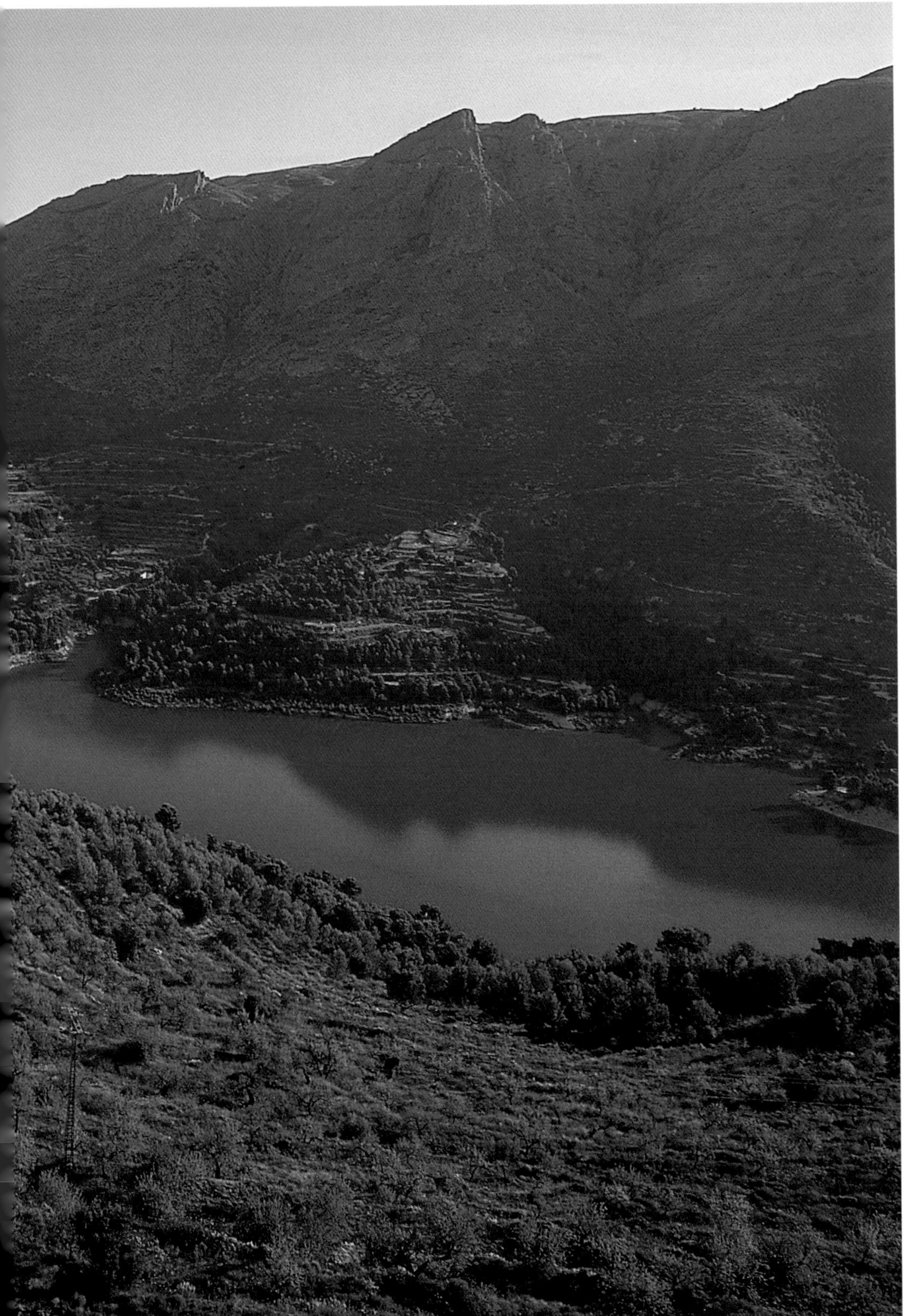

Guadalest is a real bazaar which recalls its past Moorish period. Shops that offer all sorts of products are open in the tiny urban centre, which besides has six different museums. In a typical house of the XVIII century is the Ethnological Museum, which shows us a traditional house with its bread cooking oven, living room, pantry, the farmyard with animals and several agricultural tools; even the bedroom has clothes from the period. Stand out also the Model Museum (Museo de Maquetas), the Microgiant Museum (Museo Microgigante), the Museum of Miniatures, the Torture Museum and the Museum of Old Toys.

On our return journey, 3 km before arriving to Callosa d'En Sarrià, we have to visit a place of incomparable beauty: the **Algar Fountains** (Fuentes del Algar), an oasis of vegetation, of cultivations and with an extraordinary behaviour of the abundance of water in this area: irrigated by the Algar and Bolulla rivers, to which join the Guadalest river and the small brooks of Aguas, Segarra, del Gat de Riquet and Vella, which increase the fast flow of the Bolulla river, which from its source, 10 km away, runs down from a height of 1.000 m. Different levels and cascades make of the route a very pleasant walk.

There is a spectacular waterfall, called Toll de la Caldera, which drops water from a height of 15 m and as in other pits or "tolls", visitors can have a swim in their waters, warm in the winter and cold in the summer, at a constant temperature of 19 °C, contrasting with the temperature of the environment. The place has a Water Museum and several restaurants which offer local cuisine: rice dishes, in all its varieties, the "minxos" (a kind of pie stuffed with tomatoes inherited from the Moorish), fishes and other products. Going towards Benidorm we can visit **l'Alfàs,** where the church of San José is, in the centre of the village, and a site with Roman remains in the beach of Albir. With 10.760 inhabitants, of which

Springs of Algar.
Waterfall of Toll de
la Caldera.

6.000 are foreigners of 54 different nationalities, this village extends in 15 very similar housing estates. In Alfaz is celebrated at the beginning of July a Cinema Festival each year which also celebrates open air shows at the Albir beach, next to the Sierra Helada. The sea promenade of this village is called *The Promenade of the Stars* for

being studded with the names of the famous actors that have attended the Cinema Festival. Near Benidorm, in the castle of the Count d'Alfàs, medieval tournaments are celebrated, where knights dressed up in typical costumes fight wielding their lances on their horses while the spectators enjoy their dinner.